AOB 4218

THE WORLD'␣␣␣␣␣␣␣␣␣␣␣␣␣ Solo ␣␣␣␣␣␣␣ASSICAL MUSIC

D0760469

Johann Strau␣␣

26 Waltzes, Polkas and Quadrilles

EDITED BY BLAKE NEELY AND RICHARD WALTERS

Cover Painting: Renoir, *Roses*, 1890
ISBN 0-634-03765-0

HAL•LEONARD®
CORPORATION
7777 W. BLUEMOUND RD. P.O. BOX 13819 MILWAUKEE, WI 53213

Visit Hal Leonard Online at
www.halleonard.com

CONTENTS

JOHANN STRAUSS
(Johann Baptist Strauss II)
1825-1899

Hailed as the "Waltz King," Viennese composer Johann Strauss, Jr. reigned over the light music scene of Vienna for more than 50 years, and over a family musical dynasty as well. The music of the Strauss family, particularly that of Johann, Jr., conjures images of glittering Viennese balls, with well-dressed nobility gracefully spinning across huge, crowded dance floors. That is, in essence, a fairly accurate image. Vienna in the nineteenth century was known for lavish balls. In 1832 alone, 772 balls were held in in the city. The balls were not simple dances. They often began at about eight o'clock in the evening, with dancing continuing until about midnight, when a dinner was served. Dancing resumed after the meal, often lasting until three or four in the morning. Composers churned out waltzes, polkas, quadrilles, gallops and other pieces to keep the dance-addicted Viennese happy.

The waltz was not always the domain of the nobility. In fact, in the early years of the nineteenth century the waltz was thought to be entertainment for the working class, and charged with ruining the morals and reputations of its dancers. Although his ability as a composer has never been questioned, part of Johann Strauss, Jr.'s success is undoubtedly due to his good fortune concerning time and place. He was born in Vienna, the musical Mecca of Europe, and came of age just as the Viennese nobility took a shine to the waltz. Vienna was the seat of the great Hapsburg Empire from the late thirteenth century until 1918. Generations of great composers lived and worked there for at least part of their careers, endowing the city with the richest musical culture in Europe. Among the towering Viennese composers were Haydn, Mozart, Beethoven, Schubert, Liszt, Brahms, Mahler, Schoenberg, Berg and Webern. The city cultivated concert music, but also adored lighter music. The obsession with dancing and the depth of Vienna's musical culture paved the way for Johann, Jr. to combine compelling rhythms with romantic melodies and orchestrations, bringing the waltz to its zenith.

Johann Strauss, Sr. (1804-1849), the son of an innkeeper, abandoned a career as a bookbinder to pursue his musical dreams. He put together an orchestra and began performing in taverns and inns, gathering a significant public following. Among his admirers were Richard Wagner, who called him "the magic fiddler, the genius of Vienna's innate musical spirit," and Hans Christian Andersen. Johann, Sr.'s main competitor was Josef Lanner, whose music was more lyrical and melodic than Strauss' rousing dances. Johann, Sr. was only 20 when Johann, Jr., his first child, was born. Although Johann, Jr. composed his first dance at age six, his father and mother agreed that their children should not pursue music, and directed Johann and his brothers Josef and Eduard into other fields. But Johann, Sr. drew away from his family, eventually divorcing his wife and becoming largely estranged from his children. With a mere 20 years age difference between father and son, Johann, Jr.'s musical debut, on October 15, 1844, launched his father's greatest competitor. Although the program that evening, at Donmayer's Garden restaurant, consisted mainly of original pieces, Johann, Jr. ended the evening with a piece by his father. Nonetheless, a newspaper hailed his debut the next morning with the words: "Good night, Lanner. Good evening, Father Strauss. Good morning, Son Strauss."

Johann, Sr. died four years later. Father and son had reconciled their musical differences, but then soon found themselves on opposite political sides during the revolution of 1848. Johann, Jr. took the side of the students in this conflict, a choice which would haunt his career for some years to come. After Johann, Sr.'s death, Johann, Jr. merged his orchestra with that of his father, soon dividing the ensemble to meet the ever-increasing demand for his music and his presence. He eventually had a total of six orchestras playing every night in Vienna. He would make an appearance at each venue, taking the baton to conduct a few numbers before rushing off to the next ball. He had more than 200 people on his payroll, providing endless dance music to the Viennese.

In 1854 Strauss expanded his following to a resort near St. Petersburg, Russia. He played there from May through late September for several years. While in Russia, his brother Josef, who also defied his father's wishes and studied music, handled the waltz business in Vienna. Brother Eduard also joined the family team, conducting in Vienna and eventually taking over the summers at St. Petersburg. Yet Strauss hated to travel, so much so that he would often be found huddled on the floor of his train compartment. Despite his fears and loathings, Strauss journeyed to Paris to perform at the 1867 World's Fair, also performing in London on that trip. He braved travel once again to appear in Boston in 1872, although not before making certain his will was updated to provide for his wife. In Boston he conducted mammoth performances at the "International Peace Jubilee," leading an orchestra of 10,000 musicians and a chorus of 20,000 singers. He was assisted by nearly 100 other conductors, who relayed his gestures and instructions much as video monitors would today.

During the 1860s Strauss began turning more of his conducting responsibilities over to his brothers, focusing instead on composition. Although the public demand for his dance music was unabated throughout his career, Strauss developed an itch to expand his endeavors. In 1868 he began writing operettas. Although he was clearly a master melodist and an artful orchestrator, Strauss had little theatrical sense. He was a poor judge of librettos and rarely mastered the art of writing for the theater. He wrote 17 stage works, of which only two, *Der Zigeunerbaron* (The Gypsy Baron) and especially *Die Fledermaus* (The Bat), remain in the repertoire.

In the midst of his busy life and phenomenal popularity, Strauss found the time for three marriages. His first, to singer Henriette (Jetty) Treffz, ended with her premature death. He then married Angelika Dittrich, an actress much younger than himself, only to divorce her a few years later. His final marriage was to Adele Strauss, a young widow who had been married to a Strauss that was no relation to the musical family. Both Angelika and Adele were involved in his work, collaborating on librettos and, in Angelika's case, doing publicity work as well. Strauss had to revoke both his Austrian citizenship and his Catholic faith in order to marry Adele, as his divorce from Angelika was not recognized by the Catholic church, and therefore not by the Austrian government. In his later years, the home he maintained with wife Adele was a place at which guests and friends were always welcome. The signatures in his guest book from these years included such names as Brahms, Bösendorfer, Bruckner and Puccini.

Although Strauss' phenomenal success has something to do with the place and time in which he found himself, his musical imagination is an enormous part of that winning equation. His early music is quite similar in character and form to his father's, which was rhythmically engaging and infectious. It was in the 1850s that Strauss came into his own, creating the elegant, charming, witty and opulently orchestrated pieces which came to be known as "dance poems" and "dream pantomimes." The influences of the romantic composers Liszt and Wagner, whom he admired, are clearly evident in his complex melodic developments. These are not just lovely melodies, they are tunes sprinkled with intricate rhythmic twists that mask the fact that the piece is still in a simple 3/4 time signature. Much of his music after the 1850s is compelling, often in expansive concert forms. One can hardly hear "The Beautiful Blue Danube" (An der schönen blauen Donau) or "The Emperor Waltz" (Kaiser-Walzer), without feeling the pull to dance. There is also a powerful nostalgic spirit about his best work, a longing for a lovely existence that even then may have been slipping away.

Strauss was more than a musical star. In a complex way he personified the identity of Vienna. It was said, rather derisively, that Emperor Franz Joseph ruled only as long as Strauss was alive. The composer's death hit the Viennese very personally. In late spring of 1899, Strauss conducted the overture at a jubilee performance of *Die Fledermaus*. Soon afterward he caught a cold, which quickly turned into double pneumonia. The whole city knew of his serious illness. Just a few days later, at an outdoor concert in Vienna's Stadtpark Pavilion, a messenger ran out onto the stage and gave a message to conductor Eduard Kremser. Kremser immediately stopped the orchestra. After a moment of shuffling pages the players began again, this time with different music. It was "The Blue Danube." The audience stood, men removed their hats, women wept, all of them understanding what the music meant: their beloved Strauss had died.

The Johann Strauss dynasty would long outlive its king. The family musicians, the father and three sons, had created more than 1,300 individual dances, and a tradition of music that still defines the Viennese spirit. When the world watched Vienna's millenium New Year's Eve celebration on television as the 21st century arrived, they saw thousands of couples waltzing to none other than "The Blue Danube."

– Elaine Schmidt

The Acceleration Waltz

Accellerationen

Johann Strauss, Jr.
1860
Op. 234

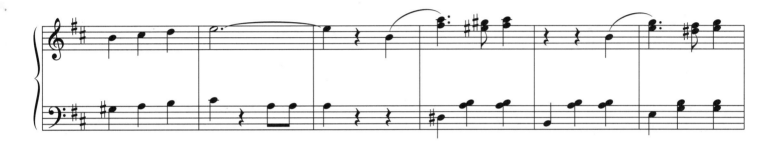

CODA

Artist's Life
Künstlerleben

Johann Strauss, Jr.
1867
Op. 316

2

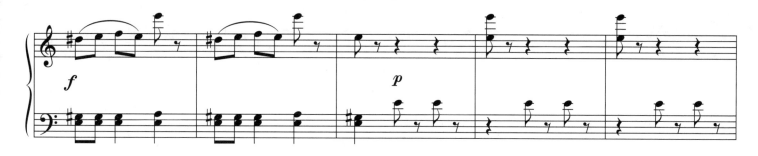

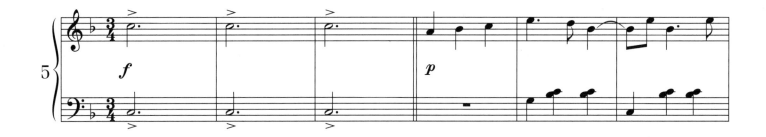

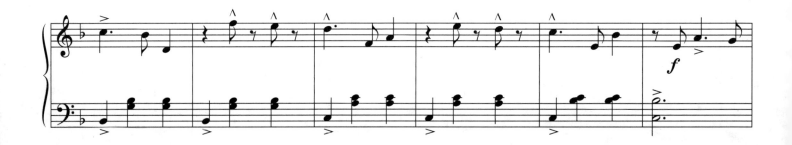

CODA

The Beautiful Blue Danube

An der schönen, blauen Donau

Johann Strauss, Jr.
1867
Op. 314

INTRODUCTION

Tempo di Valse

WALZER

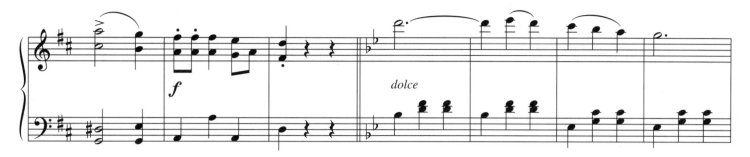

Lebhaft (vivace)

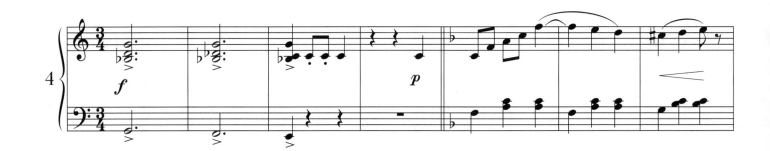

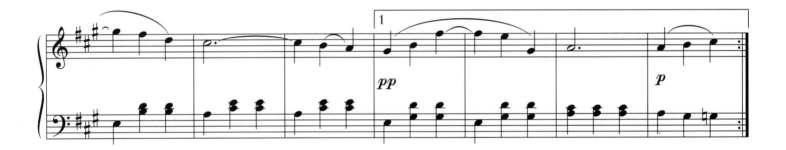

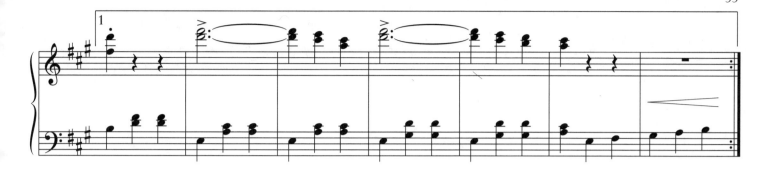

Cagliostro Waltzes
Cagliostro-Walzer

Johann Strauss, Jr.
1875
Op. 370

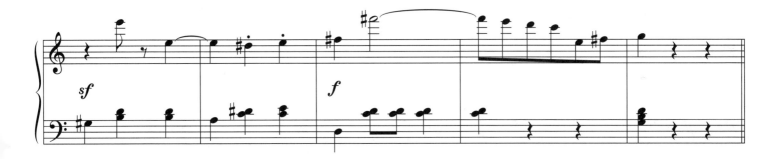

Intrada   Waltz

CODA

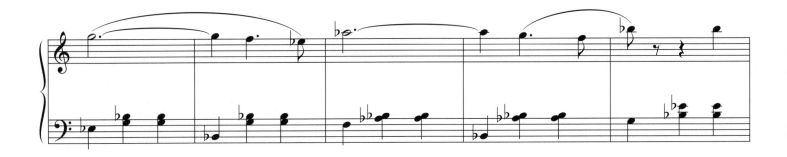

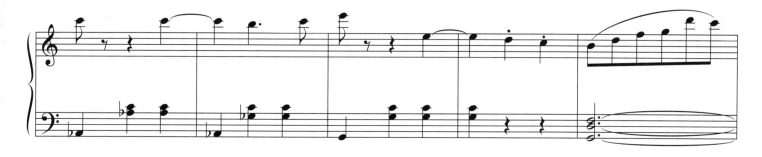

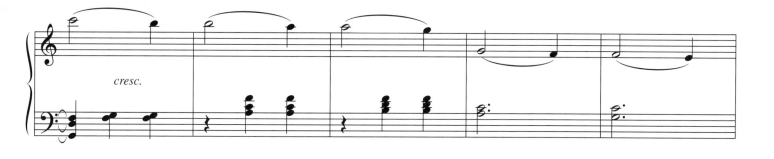

Carnival in Rome Polka

Der Carneval in Rom

Johann Strauss, Jr.
1873
Op. 358

INTRODUCTION
Moderate Tempo

POLKA

TRIO

Danube Mermaid

Donauweibchen

Johann Strauss, Jr.
1888
Op. 427

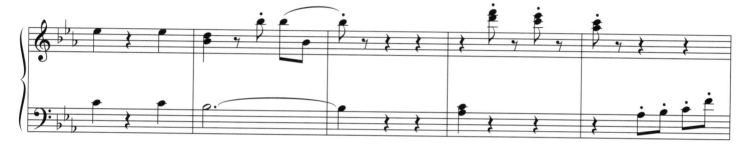

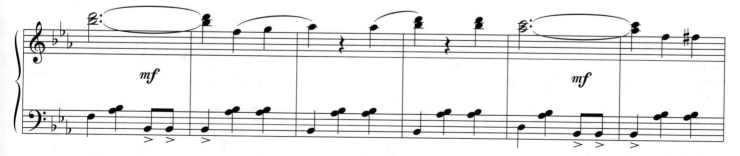

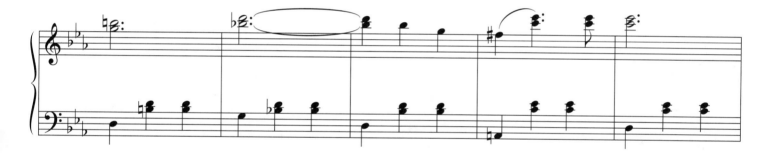

Intrada

Waltz

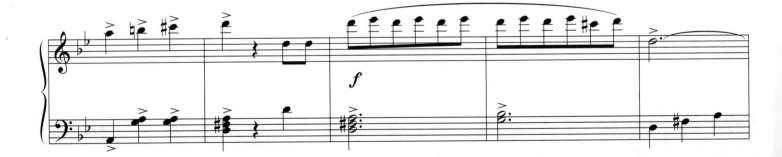

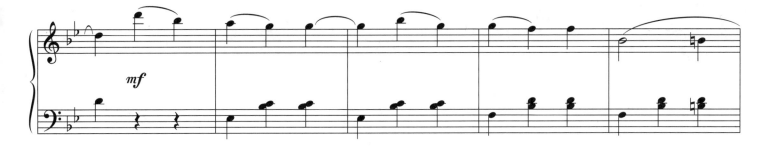

CODA

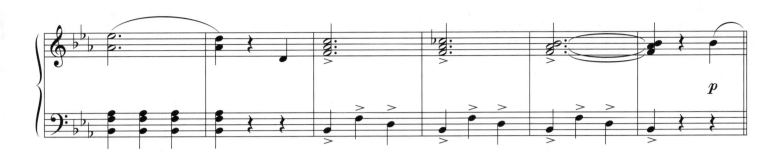

Emperor Waltz
Kaiser-Walzer

Johann Strauss, Jr.
1889
Op. 437

Slow March Tempo

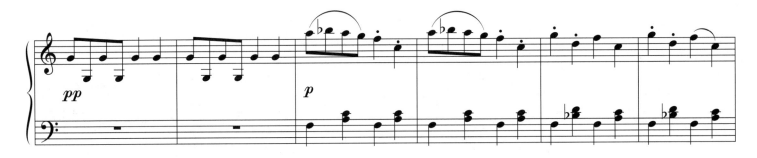

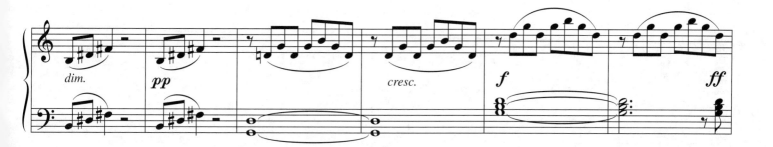

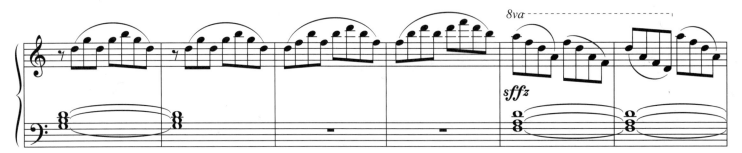

Tempo di Valse

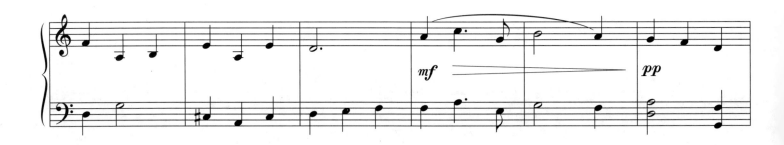

CODA

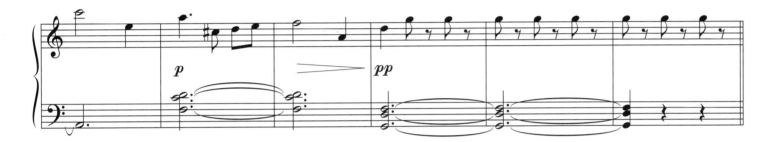

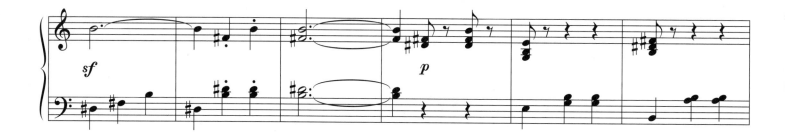

Slower

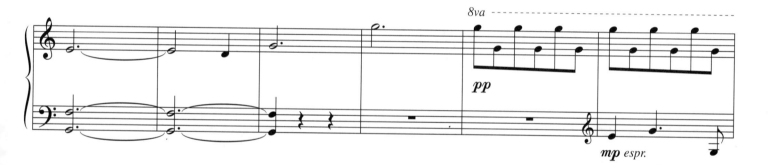

Tempo di Valse

Die Fledermaus Polka

Johann Strauss, Jr.
1873
Op. 362

To Coda $\oplus$

TRIO

D.S. al Coda

CODA

Enjoy Life

Freut euch des Lebens

Johann Strauss, Jr.
1870
Op. 340

Intrada

Waltz

Intrada

Waltz

4

Intrada

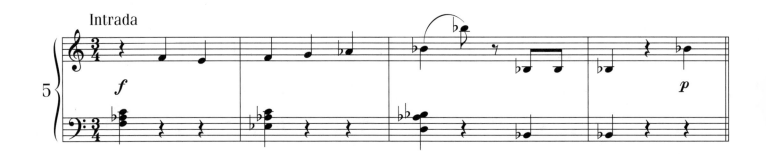

Waltz

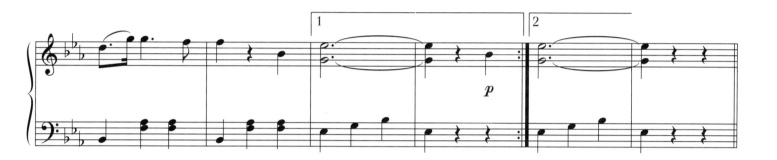

CODA

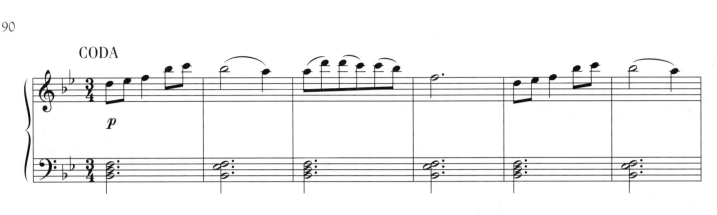

Die Fledermaus Overture

Johann Strauss, Jr.
1874

Allegro vivace

Allegretto

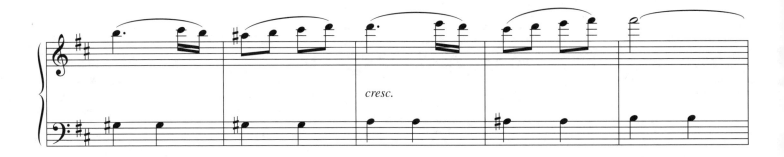

Tempo di valse

Allegro

Allegro moderato

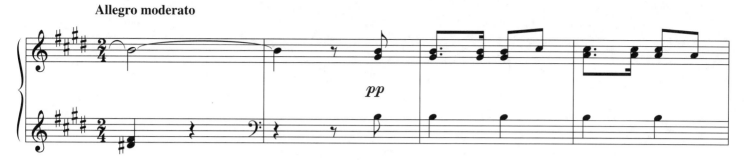

G.P.　　　　　　　　　　　　　　　　　　　　　　　　　　**Tempo ritenuto**

Tempo di valse

Kiss Waltz
Kuss-Walzer

Johann Strauss, Jr.
Op. 400

Tempo di Valse

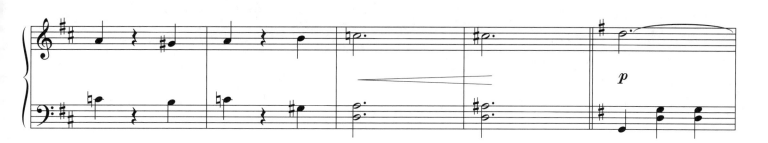

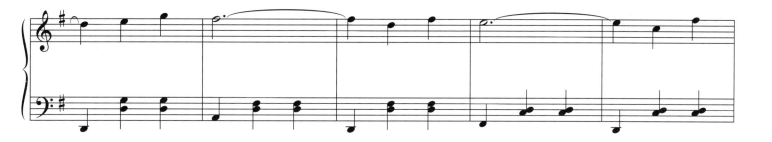

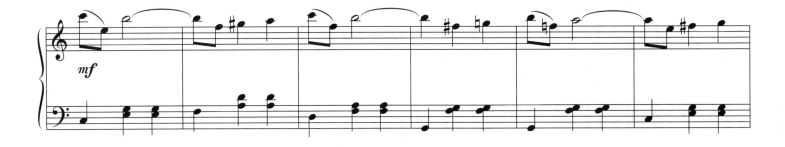

CODA

Die Fledermaus-Quadrille

Johann Strauss, Jr.
1874
Op. 363

Pantalon

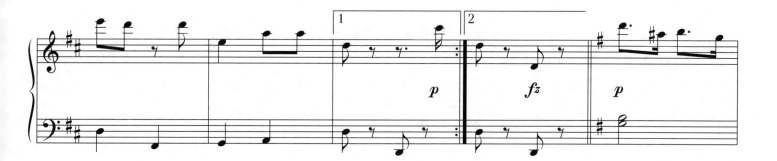

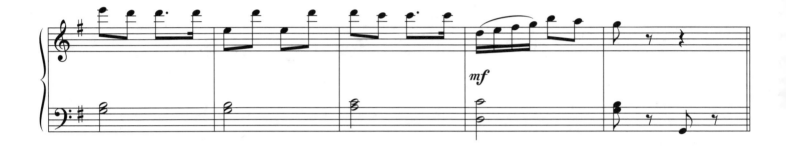

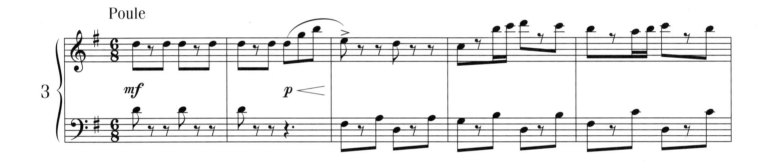

Poule

3

Trénis

Pastourelle

Finale

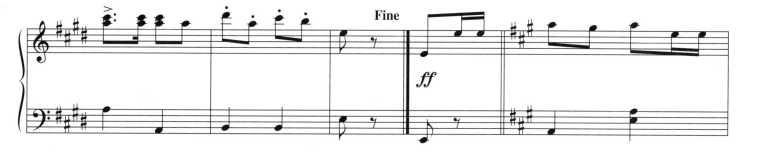

Morning Journals

Morgenblätter

Johann Strauss, Jr.
1864
Op. 279

Tempo di Valse

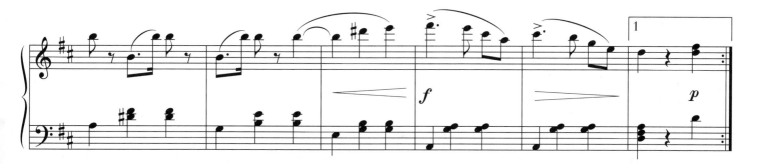

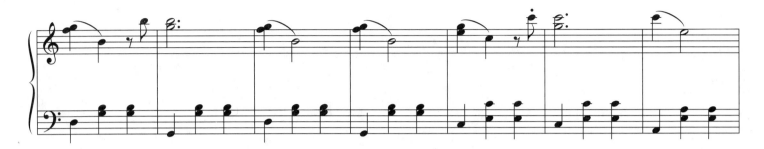

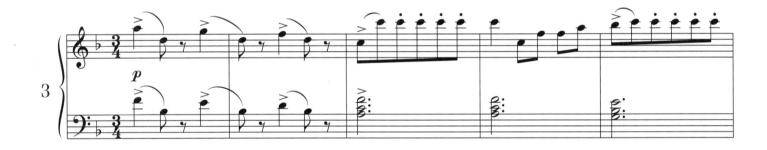

CODA

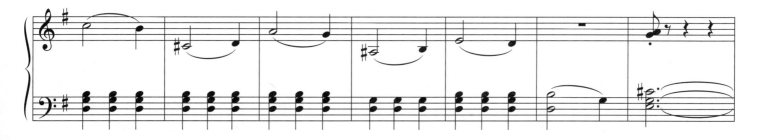

New Vienna

Neu-Wien

Johann Strauss, Jr.
1870
Op. 342

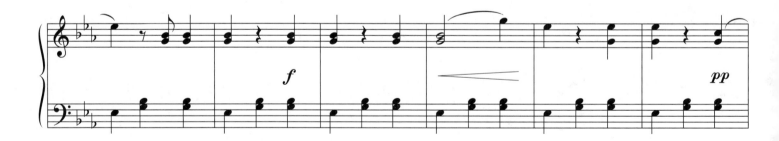

Intrada

Waltz

Intrada

Waltz

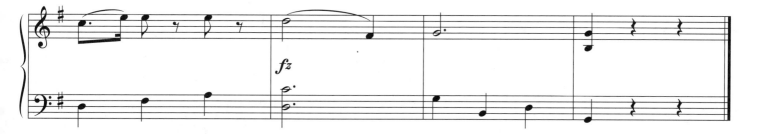

Intrada

Waltz

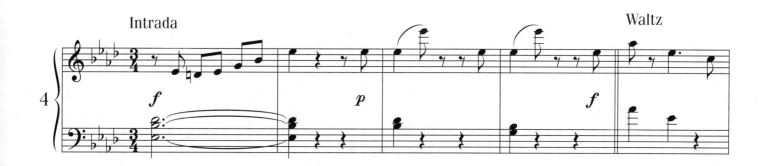

One Heart, One Mind

Ein Herz, ein Sinn

Johann Strauss, Jr.
1868
Op. 323

Intrada

To Coda

Trio

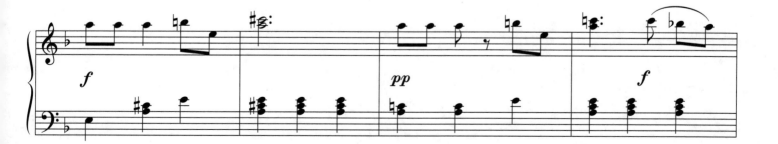

D.S. al Coda

CODA

O Beautiful May!

O schöner Mai!

Johann Strauss, Jr.
1877
Op. 375

Tempo di Valse

Fine

(To Next Strain)

D.S. al Fine

Intrada

Waltz

Intrada   Waltz

CODA

Praise of Women

Lob der Frauen

Johann Strauss, Jr.
1867
Op. 315

Intrada

Polka-Mazurka

Sweetheart Waltz
Schatz-Walzer
from THE GYPSY BARON

Johann Strauss, Jr.
1886
Op. 418

Tempo di Valse

So voll Fröhlichkeit *(Such complete cheerfulness)*

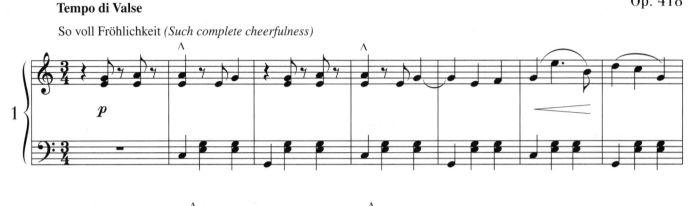

Nun will ich des Lebens mich, freuen
(Now my life will be full of gladness)

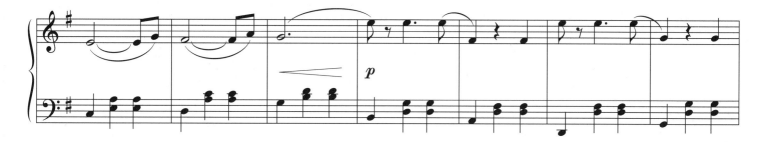

Nur keusch und rein *(Only chaste and pure)*

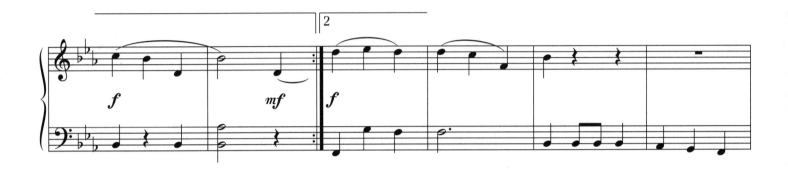

Ja, das Alles auf Ehr *(Yes, everything from honor)*

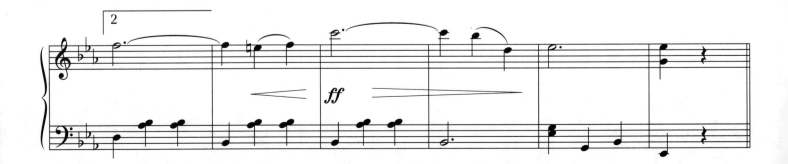

Doch mehr als Gold und Geld (*But more than gold and money*)

Das wär kein rechter Schifferknecht *(That was no proper sailor boy)*

CODA

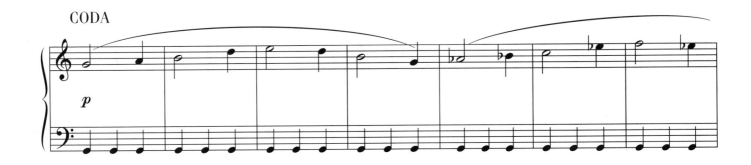

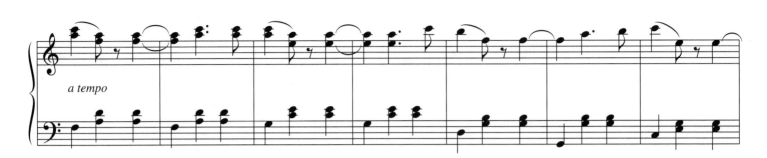

a tempo

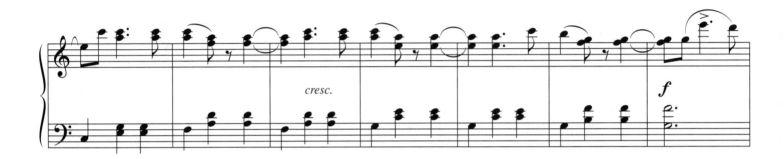

cresc.

f

f

ff

Pizzicato-Polka

Johann Strauss, Jr.
1870

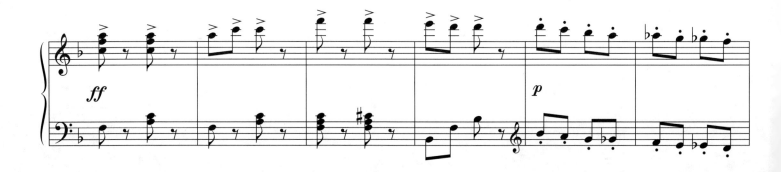

D.C. al Coda

CODA
A bit faster

Tales from the Vienna Woods

Geschichten aus dem Wienerwald

Johann Strauss, Jr.
1868
Op. 325

INTRODUCTION

Tempo di Valse

Langsam (Lento)

Moderato. Langsam (Ländlertempo)

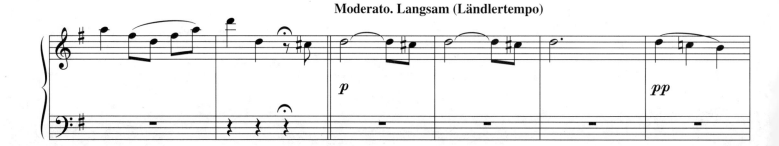

Bewegter (Più mosso)

Vivace

Tempo di Valse

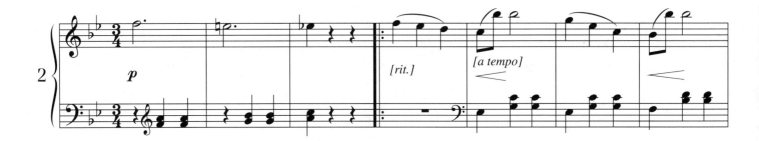

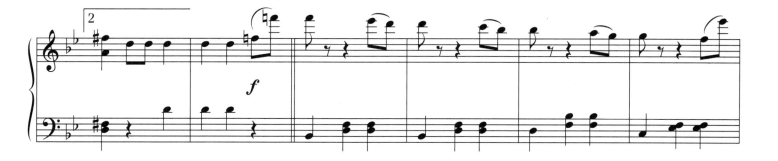

CODA

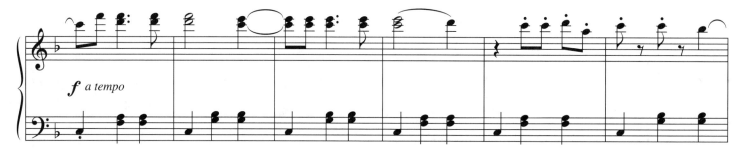

Roses from the South

Rosen aus dem Süden

Johann Strauss, Jr.
1867
Op. 388

Introduction

Tempo di Valse

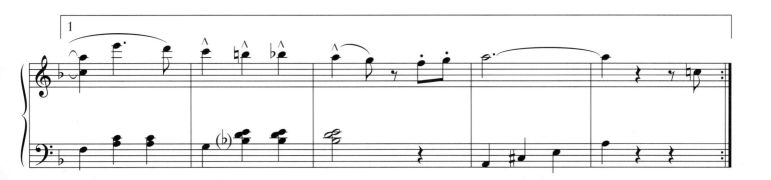

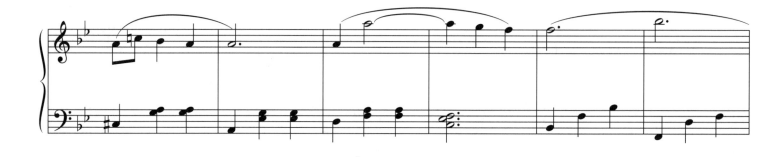

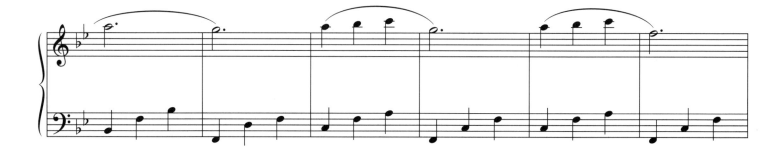

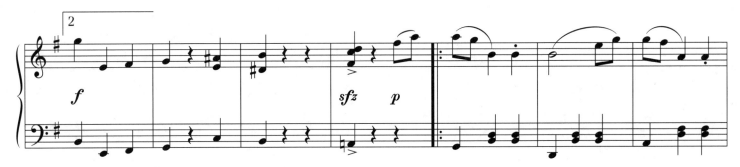

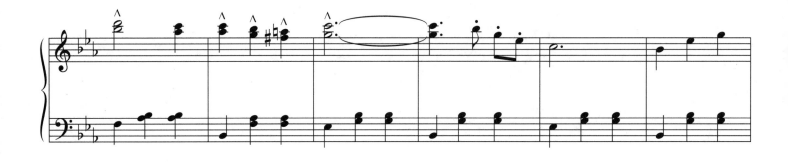

CODA

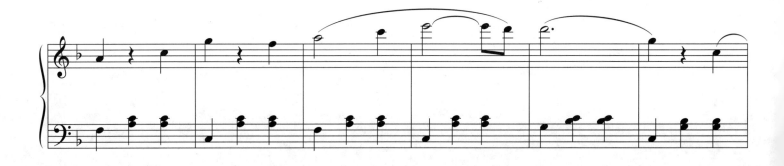

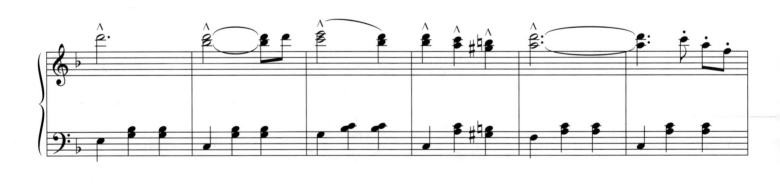

A Thousand and One Nights

Tausend und eine Nacht

Johann Strauss, Jr.
Op. 346

Tempo di Valse

TRIO

CODA

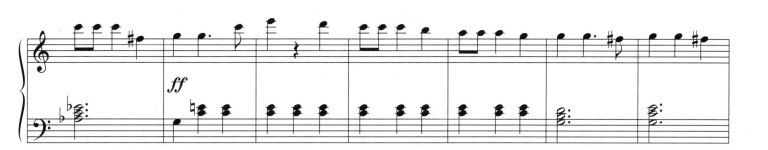

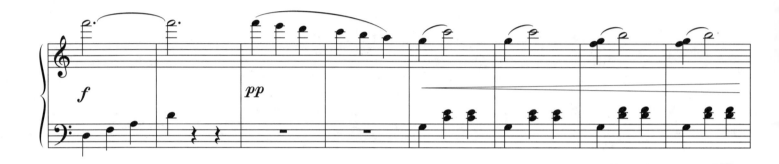

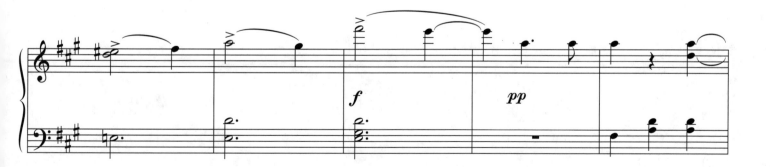

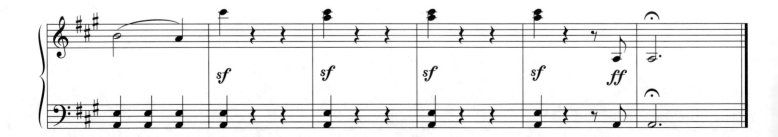

Vienna Life
Wiener Blut

Johann Strauss, Jr.
1873
Op. 354

Tempo di Valse

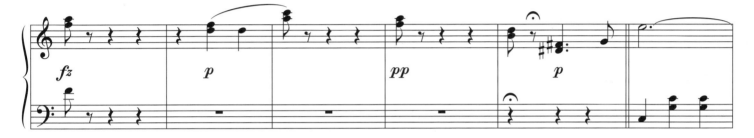

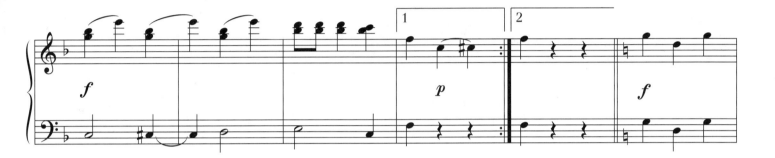

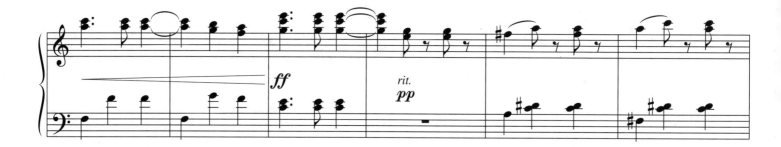

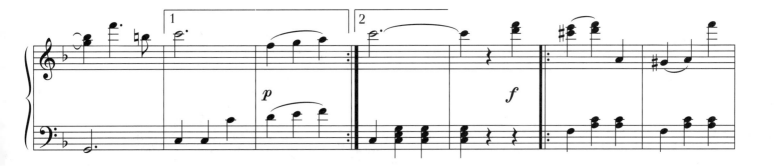

Voices of Spring Waltz

Frühlingsstimmen

Johann Strauss, Jr.
1883
Op. 410

Tempo di Valse

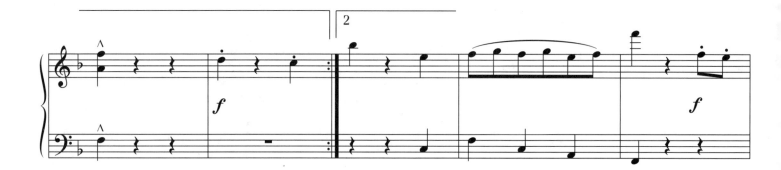

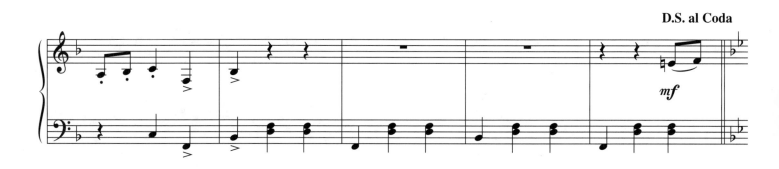

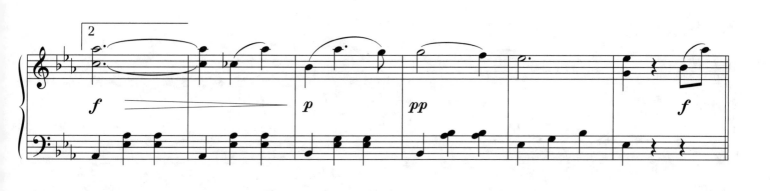

227

Where the Citrons Bloom

Wo die Zitronen blühn

Johann Strauss, Jr.
1874
Op. 364

Tempo di Valse

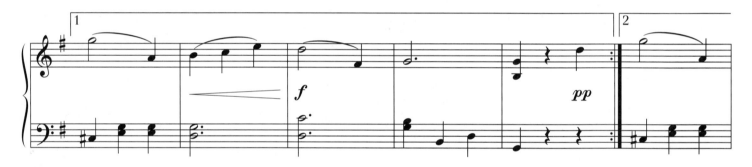

Intrada

Waltz

2

Wine, Women and Song
Wein, Weib und Gesang
(Waltz)

Johann Strauss, Jr.
1869
Op. 333

INTRODUCTION
Tempo di Valse

WALZER